The
Family

MW01658154

PROPERTY OF
CHAPTER 1 ECIA

Mr. and Mrs. Green
have lots and lots of children.

All the children are noisy.

"Why do you have
so many children?"
people ask Mr. and Mrs. Green.

"We love children," says Mrs. Green.

"Most of the time," says Mr. Green.

One day,
a girl called Joanna
comes to live with the Greens.

Joanna is very shy.
She doesn't talk or play.
She doesn't want to eat.
"Joanna is shy," says Mrs. Green
to the other children.
"Don't rush her."

On Saturday,
Mr. Green says to the family,
"Because Joanna has come to stay,
we're going to celebrate."

Joanna doesn't know
what *celebrate* is.

"*Celebrate* means
we're going to have fun,"
shout the other children.

Mr. and Mrs. Green
take the children
to the amusement park.

The man at the gate
is selling tickets.
"How many?" he asks.

"Too many to count,"
jokes Mr. Green.

The man laughs.
"Then I'll let you all in free."

The children take Joanna
on the merry-go-round.
She likes riding on the horses.

She is a bit frightened
of the roller coaster,
but she has a second ride on it.

The children are throwing hoops
to get a rabbit.
All the hoops miss.

Mr. and Mrs. Green try.
They miss the rabbit, too.

"Come on, Joanna," they say.
"It's your turn."

Joanna is shy.
She doesn't want a turn.

"Come on, Joanna!"
the children yell.

So Joanna has a turn
at throwing the hoops.

Clunk!
A hoop goes over the rabbit.

The family cheers.

Joanna shouts, "I got it!
I got it! I got it!
I got the rabbit all by myself!"

Mr. Green laughs.
"Looks like we've got
another noisy Green," he says.